POEMS FROM THE MIND SHOP

David Ashbee

Poems from the Mind Shop
© David Ashbee

First Edition November 2020

ISBN: 978-1-913329-30-3

David Ashbee has asserted his authorship and given his permission to Dempsey & Windle for these poems to be published here.

All rights reserved. No part of this publication may be reproduced, stored in a retrieval system or transmitted in any form or by any means without the written consent of the author, nor otherwise circulated in any form of binding or cover other than that in which it is published and without a similar condition being imposed on a subsequent purchaser.

Published by Dempsey & Windle
15 Rosetrees
Guildford
Surrey
GU1 2HS
UK
01483 571164
dempseyandwindle.com

British Library Cataloguing-in-Publication Data

A catalogue record for this book is available from the British Library

'The charity shop I work in as a volunteer is not
　The Mind Shop
　　　　　…but in many ways it is.'

Contents

I

"First Published 2004" …	10
An Eye for an Eye	11
Spare Time	12
October sunlight	13
Dazzle	14
Westerly — an Horatian Ode	15
Wet Rooves	16
To be…	17
Poems from the Mind Shop	18 – 22
Mind Shop Donors	23

II

Man with pipe	26
God Willing	27
Clara	28
Fairground Girls	29
Things our art teacher never said	30
The Masters	32
Cavern	34
The conductress	35
The Midlands Lodger	36
Hartley Everett on Elvering	37
For Robbie MacGregor r.i.p.	38
Roy King is a self-confessed slime-mould obsessi	39
This notice…	40
I call her Myra	42
The sign-language woman on the Welsh channel	44
The Men	45
R.S.Thomas writing workshop, Criccieth	46
Tom Warwick's book	47
The Fine Art Collector welcomes company	48

III

Sequence from the RA Summer Exhibition 2016	52 – 3
The Sculpture Garden	54
Change of Season	55

Sequence from Sainsbury Art Centre, Norwich	56 – 8
The Dance (Paula Rego)	59
In the Dali Museum	60
That Shed	61
Maritime Museum Sequence	62 – 3
Those skirts	64
View from Madron Cross	65
In a bar in Madron	66
As she tells it	67
Bolitho's	68
Penzance Pirates Record Bid June 2011	69
Mazey Day Bells	70
11th June 2013	71
Collage from a Cornish Guest Book	72 – 3

IV

Field, Chynoweth Lane	76
Field Names in Upper Berkeley Hundred	77
The Gloucester Birds	78
Clockwork couldn't do it	80
The Sighting	81
The Visitors	82
Birdsong	84
The pickers	85
The Swans	86
Poet	87
Remembered on hearing Rautavaara	88
The 14th way of looking at a blackbird	89

V

Rough day	92
Last days with Richard	93
Stormlight	94
Veterans	95
Two minutes' silence	96
Penultimate Act	97
Fencing	98

My goat-willow tree	100
Such days	102
Busy day at the Beaufort	103
Shaved	104
"How can you be sure that you are the 17th reincarnation of the Buddha?' "Certainly it is very difficult."	106
"He's better at being me than I am"	107
That holiday was card games	108
To the man who put food out for the badgers	110
At "The Bell and Gavel"	111
Vinyl Albums	112
"Silver dew on the bluegrass"	114
One Way Street	116
Markers	117
The hulks' graveyard	118
Afternoon sky in South Gloucestershire	119
November Dusk	120
Crepuscule	121
Redemption	122
Threshold	123
Notes and Acknowledgements	125
About David Ashbee	128

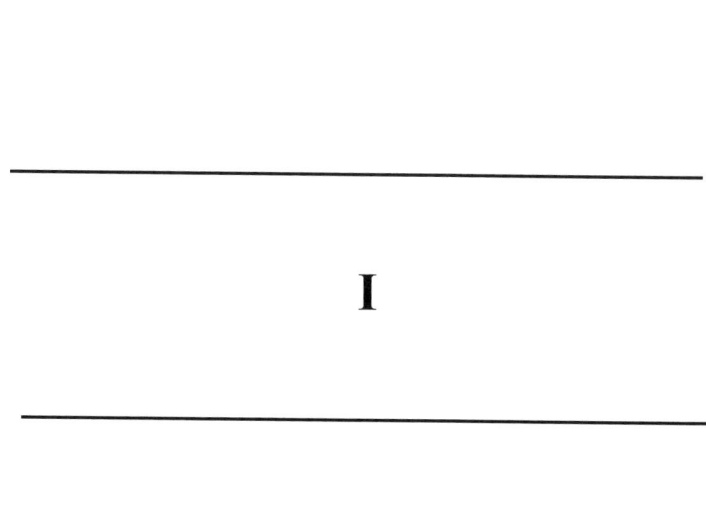

"First Published 2004" ...

...but who gave me this book, or when, is not recorded.
It was after the righting of my squinny,
but its poems were rigged before I lost my eye,
before, blind behind some muffler,
I felt them zap it out,
that lens that had slipped like a soapsud saucer,
to become the play of lasers
crimping like firecrackers on my brain.

But now they've stitched me up,
embroidered my cornea
with a tiny hall of mirrors.
Optometrists gasp as they gaze in,
breathe their warmth upon me
like eager supplicants.

A miracle of facets,
it justifies these pages,
like a wad of knitting patterns
whose basketweave and chevron
repeat or run counter as the poet's stave decrees,
to fingertip their meanings
on the nerve-ends of my mind.

An eye for an eye

Benign payback:
an eye for an eye I lost in a wood
when a tree I was torturing smacked me back.
Weeks of pain, and lying under lasers,
while such eye as remained
was bleached, folded, ironed like a shirt.

At stitching time,
I spied the fist that drew the thread,
a spider that fingered the rim of my sight —
descried it with the other eye.

Now it hangs, inside my head,
a gleaming wheel, a web.
A lens, but not the fleshy sort.
A bulb in a socket I'd feel one-eyed without.
I can't see it, though others can
who stoop and peer in
like smugglers at a cave-mouth.
I ask them to describe it,
this alien in my skull.

They show me diagrams, with arrowed lines:
how ping-pong light rays
bounce and flash like torch beams,
pixels projected on a screen,
pips that the brain reshuffles
to a goldfinch glittering on a branch
or the dazzling rink of an evening sea.

Spare Time

After my muesli I rang optometry
then unlocked the door and let in a rush
of cold garden air.
Beer-sphere and bottles to usher away.
A bowsaw grasped with already red hands
to punish the headstrong butterfly tree —
a spat between tending and carnage,
though buddleias have no flesh,
just gnarly fingers, nigh-unsnappable bone.

It was cosy coming in
to the coffee smell that wasn't even there.
Cosy to sit reading quirky words.
I'd saved a purse of small-change time to spend.
Outside the window, the buddleia sat,
a small boy brandishing his haircut.

October sunlight
(*for Zoe Avastu*)

I've got a new eye in, but October sunlight's
kind to it. I think the zigzags on the red brick wall
— a random kind of jigsaw — are a distortion
from the stitching that the surgeon wove,
He might have sat cross-legged like a tailor,
above the opaque screen across my brow
as he traded embroidery-stitch anecdotes
with his apprentice who is over here from Cairo.

But October sunlight's frank too,
and shows things as I think they are.
Mortar-sliced bricks on the angled coping
duel with railing shadows projected from the south.
Slim red-fingered leaves on the tree by the bird-table
propose a less perplexing theorem.
As I stroll home, contemplating ziggurats, interstices
and the interval between equinox and solstice,
a white cat rises from the shadow of a shed
as eye-soothing pale as last night's moon.

Dazzle

The light on the sea
this miracle morning,
a polished tray
far out,
threw sunflake confetti
that grew to a
snake's head
brewed a few minutes only
until all I could see was
a dancing dazzle

and then my hood came down

I thought I had had too much
of cloud and pewter
but after sunset's
blood and bruising
and the milky thick of night
I relish that tarnish again

Westerly — an Horatian Ode

As if my eyes had cataracts
looking through this stippled window-pane
at the garden's wreckage: shrubs broken-backed
and ragged blooms drooping, heavy with rain.
Above the smudged-out charcoal line of hills
the midday sky is a milky tinplate grey.
Debris from the woods is scattered down the lane
   as another cloudburst fills
the gutters with torrents that whirl and rush away
in fishbone and fan shapes, leapfrogging the drains.

I should be out there, tramping the woods
or picking a course across rain-sodden fields
where every gateway is a lake of mud
and the track to the hill-fort is mist-congealed.
I should be out there, but my boots, coat and cap
have suffered enough, and are utterly soaked.
Yet my heart still longs for the sea-smell, the frantic
   lashing and spiteful slap
of a roiling front that engulfs like smoke
and washes our hillside streets with the wild Atlantic.

Wet Rooves

After a misty night, a clearance;
strands of wet wool on the tree-cluttered hill.
No pool but a thin dew-manna
dimples my felt roof.
The garage's corrugated steel
spreads a fine sheen.

But what thrust a pen between my fingers was
that perennial marvel,
the triangle of slate beyond the church,
above the jumbled houses,
propped to face east like some experimenter's mirror
empty now of galaxies and moons
but pompous with light — dawn light,
a damp-after-night-mist,
pearl-grey and gleaming
Sunday churchbell light.

To be...

To be up early and find a world of people
strolling to the station with sunfire on their hair!
To shrug off bedsheets and don the cold mist
of morning, through which only birds are rejoicing!
To crest the hill at the same time as the sun
lighting up the valley floor of garlic stars
and scarcely believable bluebells,
to watch a new world pour in like water,
sparkling water, already warm to the touch,
a world full of people who too have shrugged off
duvets, ablutions, breakfast cups and crumbs,
and arrived at this platform to join me in awaiting
the alleluia of our soon-to-be-elsewhere train.

Poems from The Mind Shop

1.

Early morning in the hottest July for years
but not steamy in The Mind Shop
with the street-door wedged ajar
and the fan spinning to my cool jazz.
It sucks the punters in
to browse among the floral blouses
ice-clear glassware
holiday paperbacks jolly as deckchairs.
I'm standing tall to their attention
courgette-cool in my crisp laundered shirt
tapping fingers on the counter
in time to the clarinet
and longing for Marcia with her melon-wide smile
to breeze in
and buy up all the Outsize.

2.

Yesterday
in the rapeseed fields
a thousand white butterflies
splintering across the eyes
changing shape and direction,
a noontide discotheque.

Today in The Mind Shop
gaudy figures
flick across my sightline.
In midday blue,
crimson-rose,
pea-pod green,
white only on their wingtips,
they settle momentarily,
antennae twitching,

on shelved shoes,
cushions, albums,
cuddly toys,
making the shop a wildflower meadow,
and they exotic creatures of high summer,
sprung from shaded seed,
who fluttered in when I
flung wide the door
to fill the shop with sunlight's pollen.

3.

Sun across the street and out the back
warming the dewdamp bags left overnight.
I harry out the early clientele –
leaves blown in by traffic from the porch.
An old hand now but my first brush with the broom.

I unzip a guitar,
invent a price
and prop it in the window
with its footstool and tuner,
imagine flamenco dancers
spinning like flies;

put on some music, piano and vibes,
tunes from an autumn woodland
to match the hat display,
calling the shoppers yet to come,
and soothing me
as I plug two gaps in Fiction with
'Shadow of the Wind';

pad back to the till,
my mood vibes-mellow;
the sun has reached the threshold of the café;

a redhead passes,
her mane on fire.

4.

The Mind Shop is empty
but for sunlight and some jazz piano,
full of that vast vacancy
that cuts those who enter down to size,
as if it's been sucked clean by a vast nozzle
unclogging corners, flattening out all nooks.

I return to its shelf my skim-read
'Rough Guide to Portugal',
feeling I am back there
gazing out from Castelo dos Mouros,
not here on a repaired IKEA chair
at the Barricade of The Till.

The jazz CD
turns on its horn
as if to hallelujah
the rack of half-priced fiction.

But no-one buys;
no-one comes.
The afternoon winds away upward
into the clouds
like a funicular.

5.

The Mind Shop door's best left ajar
to suck life in like a sluice
and allow it to be
a stall on the street,
a hey y'all come bazaar

to admit the mill-race roar
of cars, trucks, scallies
hooting out of school,
and the rattling leaves they kick-box in.

Even wind and driven sleet
is better than shut silence.

6.

A man came into The Mind Shop
and talked about his bunions,
calluses, corns, whatever. He didn't name them
but with an upside-down hand like a spider
showed whereabouts on his soles they were.
He'd brine-soaked them, filed them down,
and now his feet were fine, he said,
springing up and down like I do before a game.
The snag was
those stone-hearted growths would be back;
he needed the chiropodist up our side alley,
but nobody was there.
Could be at lunch, I said.

I'd never been up there, but the foot-chap once came here.
Tickled to hear I also played a banjo.
I'd sold him some books – 'Frailing your five-string'
and 'Bluegrass for Beginners.'

I didn't bother the bunion man with this
but picked my hard-skinned finger-ends
as he made his filing motions.
The crazy thing is his appointment's tomorrow
but he wants the chiropodist to be there today
so he's sure of where to go!
If I'd said he'll be practising Scruggs rolls,
he wouldn't have understood.

Mind Shop Donors

They come in smiling, offering oblations,
explain that the shoes have never been worn —
only later those mud flakes in the soles —
and the cardigan is from M&S
which means they claim a voucher.

They need to be well thought of:
they're recycling despair.
They've packed away the hunched shoulders, grim looks,
when they faced the heaps of creased and cobwebbed "stuff".
We all bequeath or are heirs to "stuff";
Granny's gone elsewhere
or Daughter's found a fella.

Here we only see the sweet end,
when it's sorted, or sort of, or…not.
A dead moth or plastic soldier, even till receipts.
But I see their smiles expand as they dump it at my feet,
a load off their reordered minds.
They show they've "tagged the bag", as if they're in control.
It's the ones who really are that frighten me.

I watch them almost skip back to the car,
as if this stuff is their shorn locks
and they the lighter for it.
They're thinking paint and new stuff
to plug the painful gaps.
Today is the first day
of the rest of their gift-aid lives.

II

Man with pipe

In a gallery of celebrities
few of whom I recognise or know
or feel the least inclined to
there is you

with that curved crooked pipe
like a saxophone you suck
lips pursed as if to blow it —
   one   blue   note

your thin horse face emerging from
a beard streaked black and brown
a straggly stocking at your chest
wire wool your claw fingers rake

as some men scratch their heads
in momentary despair;
but judging from that look you wear
you're never fazed

eyes that gaze through wire-rimmed glasses
seem to say
whatever art you compass
is ego-warped but true

you're the artist between strokes;
those silent lips will spurt
smoke-rings of colours
when they part

I know I've met you many times
with your soft speech, your sharp stare,
but I find what unnerves me is
your tobacco sanctity

God Willing
(1959)

The new Minister was much as I'd expected:
raised eyes at the pulpit;
hands like warm wet gloves;
his chuckle like a bottle emptying.
We youth club wallahs met in his manse
for ginger nuts and pallid tea
(lemon squash for abstainers),
perched on chaises longues
or lost in sagging chairs.

What was unexpected was his daughter,
voluptuous, about our age,
whom, deo volente, weather permitting,
I'd meet elsewhere on other terms.
But God was not willing,
the weather frowned,
and her boarding-school term began.
Nothing left to say except
the family's name was Tutt.

Clara

Retired in the '50's
so it's hard to imagine
the year she came in
— to fill the dead men's shoes, they say,
and the void in herself, maybe.
But we had no empathy then.

She did let us breathe
but only to her tapping,
between barks of the nine times mantra.

A small board monitor-turned each Monday
switching "Think before you ink",
into "Look before you leap."
We never dared to leap,
hardly dared to raise a hand
to show we knew an answer,
never for the toilet.
Most boys got "the stick",
me included;
it seemed to do the trick;
none of her charges failed the 11-plus.

The day the results came out
we were bursting to tell her
the moment we heard her chugging pre-war Morris.
Along she came, handbag on cocked arm,
and as she passed us lined up by the coke heap,
"failed"
"failed"
"failed"
she sang, with seeming satisfaction,
and what we suspected for the first time ever
could have been a smile.

Fairground Girls

Screams fly over the rooftops
as their tresses stream behind them,
girls with candyfloss faces
and shining humbug eyes.

They ride the bright machine,
gripping the bar in a seizure
of togetherness,
long past the cautious age
when this was a rite of passage
they trembled to endure.

Adventure swells them now,
pumps them with its vertigo urges,
twirls them to narcotic heights
tight in the clutch of a lover without shame.

Two pound. It only costs
two pound.
They pluck them from small purses.
Their screams can be heard in the forest
on the far slopes of the hill.

Things our art teacher never said
(for all surviving members of 1 Upper)

Boys, are we going to have a ball today !

That chap at the end, move out a bit,
we artists hate straight lines.

I came here in the war to replace the men
and stayed here ever since.

If you want guidance on your homework
my door is always open.

Ashbee, with a little more encouragement
your work could be quite distinctive.

My Giddy Aunt, it's far too quiet in here.
Try to imagine a bear garden.

Tomorrow I'll bring in my boneshaker bike
and when we've had a go at drawing it
I'll ride it down the corridor, no hands.

As I'm your form tutor as well,
I think we have a special empathy.

Tomorrow, as a treat,
we'll hire a time machine
and see how Tracy Emmins makes her bed.

I like the way Jim Linnet flicks that paint.
Did you get that from Kurt Jackson ?

Why not use a bigger brush
and make a mural?

Here is a photo of Geoffrey Phillips playing his French horn.
This week's homework is to interpret it
in the medium of your choice.

Don't I look a dandy in this hat ?

The Masters

Their gowns were smudged with chalk;
teapot and ashtray taints
leaked from their folds.

One or two were seen about town,
cycling puffily up Wooton Pitch
or meekly carrying a stout lady's shopping.

But their proper place was here —
these corridors, staircases,
the cut behind the Fives courts.

Some wore overalls, not gowns,
stained and holed by lab or lathe,
but the artist wore old tweed.

Yellow-fingered, unconcerned by appearance,
he sat for hours before his most enduring work —
a two-lb jam-jar almost full of ash.

Popeye, with grey marbles in his skull,
and said to be a Mormon,
coughed ironically when peeved.

Sinker talked of "men with woolly hair"
to demonstrate why a corollary
was not always true.

A new, untrained one
stomped in unannounced
and threw around detentions like confetti,

spotted his features in bike-shed graffiti,
got fireworks through his letterbox,
and left.

The Head loved chuffer trains,
preached in chapels of a Sunday,
brayed like a donkey.

When The Gas Board rejected me
he retorted with a hoot:
"They don't know what they're missing!"

Several played rugger.
One had taught Pinter.
All left handprints on my soul.

Cavern

Even as they sat their final tests
while sweat trickled down their pens,
they could hear the music,
breeze-born through the skylights
a strain of the other world out there
as it honked and roared away.

Freed at last, they were drawn towards it.
Against the tree-dark hillside
it blared and flashed like a fairground.
Inside its tinted windows, mis-shaped figures
jerked through swirling zones of colour,
or sat hunched, sipping blood-filled straws
with shining vampire eyes.

Its door revolved like a fan,
snaring firefly girls,
ejecting staggering boys,
projecting magic-lantern flicks
of pockmarked men with bulbous snouts.

How far back into the rocky hill it plunged
they couldn't tell
until they risked its noisy gulp,
penetrated its smokescreen
to brave its swooping shafts.

How many re-emerged is not in our statistics.
But very late, some did, it seems.
And strangely changed.

The conductress

At each station the conductress
tests the temper of the train.
Her tours are 20 miles apart
but the view is always much the same.
She knows by heart the flowerbeds,
the small white regulation plates on poles,
sighs for the inevitable couple
who poignantly neck at the gate to the nether world,
but all she has eyes for is
this fanned deck of glinting panes
where we her prisoners peer out and wonder
where we are, the sentence length to go.

But she's blind even to us.
Her duties are doors,
flustered newcomers seeking reassurance
that this is the Derby train
Her signals we don't notice,
giveaways to how our world could topple.

Oh earthbound stewardess
who lost the glamorous plot,
no spotted scarf or part in a runway mime,
you are blest with terra firma,
the comfort of terrace walls and chimney pots,
wayside halts like stations of the cross.
You are all that's left
of that sacred band
of wheeltappers, porters heaving pigeon baskets,
men with show-off flags.

Despite your anxious hourly cry in uncoached vowels,
despite your mousey hair and sagging trousers,
despite your desperate pretence
that we'll be home in time for tea,
oh how I love you.

The Midlands Lodger
(*after Carol Ann Duffy*)

Sometimes, although he doesn't pray, he finds himself
standing at a bay window, gazing out to watch
the morning light as it swells over chimneys, church tower,
lines of wires and left-out washing.

A part of him that some would call his soul
is stunned to gratitude
as the band of cream-gold grows, pushes up beneath
grubby-bellied clouds
still slipping off their nightshirts.

Pray for him who cannot pray,
you farmers and fishers,
you who hunt by dawn.
Pray that the radio's tinny burst
of jingles, bleak news and Bojangles
doesn't steal him from himself, doesn't
wrench him back too soon
to a dim back room where underwear
is frothing round in a shuddering machine.

Or if it must,
pray that his eyes retain this glow,
this living sky, this moment.

Hartley Everett on Elvering

Never see um in daylight now.
Old Baldwin used to sit thur of an afternun
and ketch alfapound a shut.

Now they leaves when they should be comin'
and then some others comes.
They doan' know 'alf on it.

T'other day a chap on Weskit Bridge
said 'e wuz really into 'em.
How many was 'e getting'?

Twelve a time!
Twelve a time, I ask yuh.
What a turnip!
In the old days
you'd get 'alf a bucket a shut.

You asks me 'ow you can start
if you 'ant never done it.
If you never done it now,
doan' bother startin'.

What you'll ketch woan' fill a paper bag.

For Robbie MacGregor r.i.p.
(a found poem)

"Brigadier
Sir Gregor MacGregor
Of MacGregor,
Sixth Baronet
of Lanrick and Balquhidder
was 23rd Clan Chief of Clan MacGregor
and a Grand Master Mason of Scotland.

"He held a belief in
clanship ideals
and believed in upholding them
to clansmen's delight
all over the world.

"He maintained firm links with
The American Clan Gregor Society,
cutting a fine figure
in his red MacGregor kilt.

"MacGregor's response
when his mount broke wind
before wind and brass
was 'Sorry about that,
Brigade of Drums.'
'That's alright sir,'
a piper retorted,
'we thought it was the horse.'

"Close friends knew him as George."

Roy King is a self-confessed slime-mould obsessive.

"Slime moulds are shy" he says,
but he knows where to find them.
"The blob that ate cars was one such" he tells me
as we trek wet woods
and happen upon our Eureka place —

a piccalilli circus
where clots like overcooked baked beans
or vomited paella
pulsate and seep in a time-lapse tide,
a cordon closing in on victims.
Vile thin-spread scrambling egg
it coagulates, gesticulates —
nauseates if you're not Roy King.

Clever stuff this, that calculates while thickening —
a thousand decisions a second,
to bring up your program — bingo! — on a screen.

All this in a woodland without wi-fi.
Not so, this is the wi-fi,
this toad spawn, this gunk.

I'm beginning to smell the coffee.
I'll shake hands now, Roy King,
and wash them quickly after.

This notice...

...made me fish him from memory's litter-bin
where he'd lain unrecalled
since that single line in the local Gazette
that even the librarians missed,
though he'd not breezed in for days,
hailing them loudly by their given names
and turning heads at computers.

He usurped my title once
when he first appeared in town,
ordering from our school supplier
Shakespeare editions we didn't require,
and the shop assumed he was me.

His neighbours came up with a nickname
— Coco the Clown —
perfect for those ski-length brogues,
bewildered eyes and rubber jowls.
Later he was Richard,
in the library at least.

Then he became The Dog Man,
ineffectually wrenching
beasts as big as himself
off quivering yelping pooches
until a court appearance deprived him
of his sad slavering friends.

But here now, on this notice
taped up 10 degrees cock-eyed
in the window of the Over-60's Club,
scrawled in biro
on ragged paper torn from a pad

is an invitation for all and sundry
to his funeral at St James,
and something that someone somewhere
must have known all along:
his complete three-part name.

I call her Myra

Only now can the truth be told — now
when the party concerned has moved on again
to another town, with yet another hairstyle.

But I swear I knew her, was without doubt
the first man she was intimate with
since her spiriting-away.
I feel proud that she could trust me,
though I admit I didn't love her.

Curiosity drove me on.
And I doubt very much whether she loved me.
Her affairs with other men made headline news.
After such exposure, what forgiveness?

I needed to let her know I'd penetrated
her disguise, alias, well-rehearsed alibis.
"Trust me," I pleaded, "trust me."
But how could she trust anyone
when women twice her weight
had been besieged in her name
from Walthamstow to Whitby?

"I'm genuine, Myra," I whispered as we lay together.
Her eyes widened; she tensed.
"Why call me that?" she said.
"That's not my name."
Of course I knew that
But she must have got the reference,
become an expert on codes.

I guard with my life the note she left.
Not until she's dead will anyone see it.
Certainly not The Press — those hypocrite moral guardians,
those... vermin.

Call me if you like an Unreliable Narrator.
I hardly know myself.
How can A be A when A is B
all the way from Walthamstow to Whitby?

The sign-language woman on the Welsh channel

Do they speak Welsh on Skomer?
The puffin's bill is full of fish;
it lifts a threatening wing.

This is an island race
on the fringe of an island race,
a bracket tongue in brackets.
Only winds are loquacious here.

I talk neither their language nor hers,
if she can be said to talk at all.
But she shows which way the wind blows,
with her frowns and puffin cheeks
while counting on her fingers.

Oh cariad of the corner,
with your semaphore and flowing locks,
waft me back to the mainland
with its M-way hub and forked-tongue Web.

The Men

When I swung back from the toilet
I missed the flash of feminine thigh,
blonde hair splayed across the headrest,
the alluring whiff of perfume.

The train was full of single men,
each sprawling in his bay, unshaven.
Flickering evening sun
threw shadows of their stubble,
made pits of their nostrils,
pink tired eyes.

Rumpled executives,
students, pierced and hirsute,
slumped like refugees.
They gazed at me as beasts from cattle-vans
weary of this swaying limbo
that whisked them out of London
to the tawdriness of home.

But you're a man, I told myself.
Or was I some Tiresias on patrol?

I rode their gauntlet back to my seat,
a film unspooling,
a gallery of Fellini extras,
staring, sneering, mute.

I was on the Train of Men
and would never get off.

R. S. Thomas writing workshop, Criccieth

Did he ever journey here, I wonder,
to have his bardish hair cut,
buy black ink for his pen,
or dampen his socks by the soul-chilling sea?

That could have been him,
there on the castle's battlements
watching clouds' shaggy eyebrows
lower shutters on October's fitful light.

Did locals greet him heartily
or cross to the narrower pavement
as he strode in his blowing coat
down Hen Lon to the shore?

He'd eye me askance, a scavenger of his culture,
as I riffle through menus, tariffs,
brews whose names I can't pronounce,
in search of Burton ales.

Perhaps his ghost was here with us poets,
watching scornful or bemused
as we passed round what could be hymn sheets
and picked the ribs off his old song.

Tom Warwick's book

The cover says the author is Tom Tipper
but the title page comes clean —
a coy attempt at anonymity.

He never told his live-in mistress
he'd embarked on such a venture
and it seems she didn't know
despite it being The Week's Rude Read
on the Dick and Deirdre Show.

Perhaps he was embarrassed
by the cover's titillation
if not by the thesis
(a brainwave of his own)
that men and women most resemble frogs
in a few obscure but significant sexual postures
(sketches provided, done by Tom himself.)

Essentially of course it was an academic work
with reference — though no footnotes —
to Darwin and Disraeli.
Chapter headings were as various as
"The reptile in us all"
and "What studying mating frogs
can do for impotence."

Most of Tom's friends were given a signed copy,
except the traffic warden Esme
whom Tom had once offended
by snatching her cap and trying it on
while posing in a pouch.

Mine I got at St Peter's Hospice sale.
(These things get around.)
It has wine stains on the cover
and several more dubious marks inside

The Fine Art Collector welcomes company

"Close the door. I want to keep the birds out.
One got in the other day, damned thing.
What do they call them here, those red-arsed warblers?
Well, if it dies it dies.
Too many fine things to get bird shit on.

The dog's bad enough — laid three fat poos
on the newly varnished boards
and piddled everywhere.
But he's very old,
won't be around much longer.

Anyway they'll have to be re-done.
Can you see, it's the wrong colour.
Disgusting, makes me sick to look at.
I'd rather have dog turds
than the wrong tone of varnish on oak.

They're a pain in the arse.
I'm sorry to say it, my dear —
I know you like the Frogs —
but that carpenter guy is a rancid midget.
I shan't use him again.

And look out here. No doorstep.
I tore it out, it was
offensive on the eye,
so now the rain pours in
like a spring tide in San Marco.

I need to build another
but their wood here's all wrong,
and I can't afford to import more from Toronto
unless I cash in shares
or call some favours in.

Hark at them out there!
Bloody accordions, wailing away until midnight.
I'm closing the gallery up and off to bed.
I want no part in this.
Imagine — *moules* and *frites*!

It's only just started but I've had it
fête fête fête up to here.
I'll see you tomorrow for *aperitifs*
if I haven't slit my wrists."

And he rises to give her a kiss.
    .

III

Sequence from the RA Summer Exhibition 2016

(i) ***The Pink Room***

She says she was blown away
by *The Pink Room*.
I'm never blown away.
My feet are always on the ground,
even nailed to it maybe.

Is it good to be blown away?
Don't they always come back,
those boomerang people,
back to earth with a clunk?
Even if they land in a tree,
consider that mad scramble down.
They can't hang-glide the storm wind forever,
they have to come back some time
if only to tell us they were blown away.

I was granted a glimpse
of the Pink Room on TV.
I have to confess
it didn't do much for me.

(ii) ***Spyre***

Here is footage of birdshit arriving at the Summer Exhibition.
Birdshit is what summer's all about.
Here it's encumbered by the giant horn of steel
that it's a cuckoo's egg upon.
Horn when on a low-loader
but a spire when erected, a spying spire,
a cuckoo in the nest that will project you,
splatt, onto the Burlington façade,
so that you too become birdshit
on the red cheeks of summer.

(iii) **Prize-winner**

Think redwood, bleeding sap,
the stain of stigmata.
He must have loved it
but he said it didn't work.
So he edged it towards charcoal,
didn't say why except that
redwood seeds need fire to make them fly.
He must have thought that afterwards,
after the incendiary urge,
because that's how artists are:
they find a match and then the words.
We poets start with words
then find an urge to match.

Like it or loath it, it won big bucks.
Because it's big and black, he says,
made out he was joking.

So begin with stuff,
burn it, slice it,
just like liver,
finish up with matchwood words.
We all do it, poets too.
All can have prizes.

The Sculpture Garden

Nature here has upstaged Art.
On the sleek bronze plinth
mica pebbles, glinting, smoothly rounded
draw my gaze downward
from what I'm meant to see.

Pebbles only for a moment,
a trick of Nature's artifice,
for these are raindrops
drawn as filings to a magnet,
forming quicksilver spheres
that give back the sky.

I stoop and finger them.
Dimpled for a second
they resume their perfect form,
make no attempt to roll away,
cling to the warmth of this bronze base
under autumn sun.

In the corner, by the gate
that leads me back to cloisters,
another work's upstaged:

from a ragged hedge
across to the rough-hewn gullet
of Concept 43
a spider has slung his high-wire thread

and spins there,
an artist,
unaware of all this stuff
and me.

Change of Season

It was so cold last night
that my half-finished painting
slipped from its moorings
and lay slantwise like a boat
abandoned by the tide.

It's a painting of a tide,
an estuary tide, faint line
among others, across which
burnished rays of orange
lie slantwise
like planks drifting.

I felt the cold's tide
seeping in last evening
in the sculpture garden
where planks of bronze
held interlocking blocks
slantwise
like a half-built engine-house.

It's warmer now,
my hands more secure
on the slanting pen
as I plane the wood of the page
the tide of ideas
sparkles with sunrays
and the engine-house
I have built from it
lumbers and thrums —

a poem, slipped from its moorings.

Sequence from Sainsbury Art Centre, Norwich

(i) **Just a study for…**

never keen on Bacon
but this fried egg hat
goes pretty well

might be mushrooms
in that night field
of spear-sharp leaves

that he's plugged into,
this scarecrow
with nostrils of a horse

a full moon somewhere
to glaze that scumbled hat
though it's not a starry night

no wonder he's morose
asking where they've gone
here it says it's just a study for him

so walk into the next field
he'll be there
stroking the closed-down sunflowers

scared that when they open
the stars will disappear

(ii) **Unique Forms
of Continuity in Space...**

is better to my mind
than *Confusion*
or *Soul in Hypertext*

as a title

as art I couldn't say

a title that discourages
the Find Aunt Milly game
that lets you just drink
the gold light on its flanks
hurt your eyes on its sharp points
even want to drop a marble down
or stroke it like a cat arch
which would set a flunky running so
just soothe it with your mind

stroll round it

on the third side
Ajax bronzed perhaps

find some groove or sweep
that dares you to pluck
a plum from the word box
slalom swarthy svelte

how it refuses words
they run off it like rain

it's *con tin*
uit
y in
space
uni
que
forms
there
of

the inscription says

it ought to know

(iii) **Untitled**

I am frog-green and lost.
                         Framed by my space but

     overlooked.
               When first retrieved I was
                                       call it

    content,
            suave in their palms
                                as
they passed and fondled me.

Here now for all of you to see
                      hunched on my tiny
plinth

       with sorry eyes
I feel your gazings sweeping past
          to other masks
              and mugscapes,
                                hear
you talking over me
                      the small
breeze of your gestures,
your laughter at the blurting tongue
                    of one nearby beside
me,
                    another doing
pressups,
                            an
ostentatious skull.

Seldom do you rest a gaze on me.
                  I am, for the record,
exhibit 143.

The Dance (Paula Rego)

The longest day of the year,
even the moon is up for it early —
like these people
twirling on the sand
stepping around their own shadows
that lengthen or shrink
or melt into one
but point always the same way.

Their clothes are from another era,
not ballgowns or beachwear,
but trousers with turnups and skirts that swirl.

A band could be playing but we can't hear it.
The tune must be one they all have by heart.
I feel if I heard it I'd know it too
though not the words
— if there are words.
Their lips don't seem to move.

Shall I join their dance?
Can I join their dance ?

And what would it mean if I did?

In the Dali Museum

Under glass, two floors below,
figures move through sunlight,
accomplices in this splashed charade.

The stairs are winders
where girls' legs
pistoning through short skirts
operate imagination's treadmill
as they ascend to cloudy ceilings,
their chubby street-soiled feet
bulbous as their breasts were when
they leaned into my window and
spoke in many tongues.

Now they model
for the zones they're figured in:
Cadaques, Velasquez, Cadillac —
fat tyre black and feather-duster blue.

That Shed

Everyone who comes here
knows
the body that's not here.

They see him screwing up
those
crumpled scraps of poems, is it?

covering the floor with failure,
before
going down the pub.

Is that a failing too?
You're
too polite to say so in his shed.

It's better somehow, him not here,
but
he can't be, dumb and dead now

nigh on seventy years, so why not
shut
the door on his shrugged-off space

that's a sort of mausoleum, and
go
away from here yourself, leaving this place

to the sunslant-scribbling water through the
window
drafting rhymes you can't uncrumple

when like him
you
simply are not here.

Maritime Museum Sequence

(i) Tidal Zone

They told me it was good down here. It's cold.
Bass and mullet twirl behind the glass
like mounts and jockeys circling at the stalls.
I'm solitary in an underwater lighthouse,
the dreary slosh of waves outside.
Inside, red button diagrams of wrecks.
The diver with lead boots waiting to be hung.
Time to take the lift up to dry land.

(ii) The Look-Out

Right up in the sun's face, more to see:
almost the whole town.
The harbour I've been flirting with all week
seems bluer here, the rows of masts more arty.
But it's the terraces I turn to, on the hill,
pastel-coloured dominoes with chessmen for chimneys;
the other way, a grand hotel, like a lunatic asylum;
Jen's two-coach train retreating from the station,
beyond the moist fields of Restronguet.

A gesturing guide is talking about dredging
to five out-of-season stragglers he's gathered in his fold.
When his arm returns landward, I duck and sneak away,
regretful that I haven't sketched the clouds.

(iii) **Main Hall**

Spinnakers, jibs and rollocks don't mean much to me,
regattas more so-whattish than gymkhanas.
I could be wooed but not like this —
sails without bellies, oars without creaks,
no tide or wind to swing these queer fish round.
Craft strung from the ceiling are too constrained to speak —
no splash, no spray, no slapping.
Boats' only raison d'etre
is their frank and sensual love affair with sea.

(v) **Bishop's Rock**

So here I am in the lighthouse
playing Scrabble with myself
while a pork chop on a plate
waits beside the stove.
Too rough tonight to crank the gramophone -
its needle keeps surfing on the grooves;
nowhere I can gather tinder,
no use asking who's that at the door,
just a block of flats collapsing.
Whisky bottle half-full in the cupboard.
I have no choice but take it on the rocks.

Those skirts

Such voluminous skirts they wore
with their aprons and shawls
as they sat outside on steps

peeling apples, gutting herring, mending nets,
and always by a basket
big enough for Moses.

Pickled in the lanes of lost content,
barely a ha'penny to scratch their backsides with
but they knew the art of living

and show it for us now in Penlee Gallery:
That was up The Digey
where Cocky Hawkins cussed his wooden leg.

View from Madron Cross (Richard Pentreath)
Penlee Gallery, Penzance)

A ruffled bed of sun-tanned moorland,
cloud-cooled near-ground, with crooked skulls of rock,
throws into relief three more distant:
St Mary's well-proportioned tower,
sea-lapped St Michael's Mount,
and a fan of walls that fence the light
from courtyards deep in shade,
a fort amid a wilderness,
its iron bell-tower black.

We now have views that skew Pentreath's perspectives.
That place has not survived
and all it represented we have tried to sweep away.
But an artist who once lived there
produced scenes more feeling-soaked
than Pentreath's ever were.
A short note in the guidebook
fizzes like a timebomb:
this is the asylum where Alfred Wallis died.

In a bar at Madron

He's throwing darts on his own,
right foot angled to the oche,
arm and eye cocked,
as three arrows on the same trajectory
chunk chunk chunk into the board.

Is this rehearsal for the local league,
a sort of nervous twitch,
an itch, an obsession,
or something he just does,
to slow the flow of bitter down his throat?

I couldn't do it, nor anything like it,
chip ball after ball across a practice tee,
or slam ace after ace at an imagined silhouette.

My obsession is the dog-eared map
that lies on the table before me
from which I have taken uncertain paths
through bog and bracken moorland
to find myself back here
where now I take an unmarked track
across a blank white page
armed only with a sticking pen
and the vaguest of notions
that somewhere it will out.

No known outcome
such as double-top or faultless spin.
I focus on the figure of a man
aiming his darts at a punctured board
as a thread to unravel,
knots, breakages and all,
until fingers ache, my mind is lost
and I'm scratching out bad adjectives
long after he's snapped shut his box
and gone crowing to the bar.

As she tells it

The Three Brothers Rocks were her limit
and when the soot came down
like black sea-fret
along with the flying-saucer lid
that popped up from the gasworks
Auntie thought that Joan
was buried — with The Brothers.

From the far end of the beach
on Man's Head Green
Joan had seen the bomb
dive headlong on the houses,
where Auntie should have been
drubbing the refugees' clothes
with Reckitt's Blue.

The beach's barbed-wire zone was where
they flung their arms in greeting,
having thought each other lost.
"I don't want to stay here"
howled Joan, distraught.
"I want to go to Canada."
Why there ? —

something she can't explain
over sixty years on
in the morning light of Perigord
with all the breakfast things set out
as on the hob brown newlaid eggs
sit ready for unlidding.

Bolitho's

I wonder if there are any Bolitho's
near Perranzabuloe.
Gulval churchyard's lousy with 'em,
though I don't know about Ludgvan.
'Tis said that Jim Trevorrow of Perranorwurthal
married a Fanny Bolitho at Zennor
and was buried a dozen years later at Towednack.
Some do blame a rockfall,
some the knockers or nuggies.
Some blame a broken heart,
and claim he was a cuckold,
but there are no horns on Towednack tower.
'Tis said he dropped dead on Woon Gumpus,
not far from Chun Quoit,
with his fuggan still half-chewed.
Another Bolitho, George,
sailed a lugger from Porthgwidden.
I've only met one in the flesh
— on his bookie's booth at Bath
the day my maiden filly got pipped
   by a nose on a double carpet.

Penzance Pirates Record Bid, June 2011

A pirate comes out of the bar,
puts his pint by mine,
and rolls a cigarette.
I pluck up the nerve to tell him
he's left the price-tag on his hat —
it's dangling by his right ear.
"Eh wat?" he squawks, and tears the bleeder off.
That's when I see his glossy hair's attached.
"Not bad, mine, izzit, for 9 pown."

But he's more of a pirate than those girls are,
who have gone to some lengths as stitched-up buccaneers.
He's leathery and wrinkled
with an ear-ring he might sport all the time.

Pirates everywhere today —
threading through the crowd as the first school troupe appears
with learning assistants and catering operatives
waving whale-sized paper fish aloft
on decorated poles.
One tot hoiks up her sagging skirt
and there's a whoop
from Kieron's step-mum next to me.

A band is approaching — parp parp oggie.
Another clutch of hearties — wobbly grannies these –
perhaps the Gulval W.I.
Tomorrow they'll all gather at the harbour,
every neckerchief accounted,
and blast the Hastings record back to sea.

Mazey Day Bells

I give thanks for foxgloves
in rocky Cornish lanes
unfolding each June to trump
the scowling wrinkled nettles.

Cow-parsley's scoops of clotted cream
congeal by now,
their May Day dance grown weary.
Trees in dowager skirts
are feeling their age.

But the sunburn pink of foxgloves
makes the verges hymn again.
From seams in granite walls
they lean their straw-thin stems
and reach to touch you;
their freckled silken lips pout peekaboo.

Swifts are fine, and swallows,
scribbling on vellum blue their snappy mottoes;
clouds constantly delight me,
flinging on gaudy scarves for their sunset promenade.

But these have had their due of praise.
It's foxgloves
that the Penwith bands resemble
as their horns acclaim
the season of Goljowan.

11th June 2013
(in memoriam George Conway)

You are dead and I am here
slurping Spriggan Ale
after coming in through drizzle
along St Michael's Way.

From a cabbage field's mud gulley,
fringed with cow-parsley
and scowling dark nettles,
the view across Mounts Bay was misty grey –
as if ash were falling, a tear-wet ash
that seemed to sear my face.
So hood up, like a pilgrim, I ploughed on.

Now here I sit
in the snug of an oak-beamed pub,
supping Cornish dew.
Six months ago, I was
struggling for breath,
unable to stand.

But the one that got lost
in the swirling mist
was you.

Collage from a Cornish Guest Book

(i)

Mentally the bucket is cleaned of stuff,
head and heart clarified, all nail-biting done.

No doctor but a daughter;
her recipe — she loved.

I am Hercules in retirement, glowing,
not the squid-white maggot I was.

Faces of friends I laughed with once
flock in circles on the tide.

A cello plays soft triplets;
the cuckoo year has flown.

(ii)

Predominantly it is energy gets us here.
Ladders stood against the mountain peak
where spaceships dock momentarily.

Perfect fun.
Chasing the chicks a new comedy.
Collision of cool tits
like chuffed seagull chasing mackerel.
Fish pepper the branches.
Posh room in hospital soon, babe.

I slam the piano;
a spasm of spent music
like colourful liquid grass
or watercress in blossom.
Thank you for the axe, Gerry.

Certainly an experience.
After this upheaval I rested,
avoided chapel,
cleaned the cows' chamber,
laughed at my demons,
painted my dinosaurs blue.

(iii)

Girlie, how fluid you are: a kite
in a gale; a seal, dancing;
a gannet diving,
a splosh of surf;
a bomb.
Perky, you are perfect,
incapable of stay.

Left restful you become
a mist-shower,
a campfire seen through branches,
a shady corner's snowdrops,
the warm wine smell of mint.
You are toad tracks through the fir-cones;
your art is the art of water.

IV

Field, Chynoweth Lane

No-one would call it charming, this field beside your house.
Once it was a human field,
growing stuff we needed,
stuff that changed with subsidies and skies.
Now it's just a paddock;
two horses chomp unheeded at the lower end.

A bristling field today,
a whistling zone of pigeons using it for time trials.
Wind in their pink-rimmed eyes they chase
each other, turn and return, victory
tokens in their beaks.
On the far nettle-and-tree-dark side,
clots of elderflower burn the mind's throat
with a pollen fizz.

It suits this grey and breezy morning,
a wind-chopped sea of grasses
beaded with dawn rain.
Tufts stand up like a boy's thick hair
that his hand's raked through,
tufts in a barber's grasp.

Long may this field resist the scythe,
or some clanking thing brought in God knows how,
bladed and barbarous.
The lane gate, long out of use,
hosts a rust and concrete installation,
stewarded this year by a stand of purple foxgloves.
Beyond your stout white garden wall
looms this dense hands-up terrain;
for your neighbour's cat a stalking, killing zone.

Field Names in Upper Berkeley Hundred

Rapsey Tandley Nutstock Norn
Twitchins Ruggbagge Sibley thorn
The Haw the Hale The Yoke The Freeze
Clamber Hole and Clover leaze
Pudding Pie mead & Alehouse hay
Muttonhole House and Hanging lay
Horsemarsh Haystall Hunger hill
Cowpen Cloudcrofts Kimley Well
Deepmoor Droughleaze Drywarth Dunmites
Wagbag Wild perry Stamylode Snite
Dickley Dingle Driple Down sleight
Jacks smacks Moneymines Farthing gate
Bastard hedge Brewers leaze Blacklands The Bags
Sour pit Side splot Wet splatt The Quags
Swardley Targus Hackhill Hale
Elvers Snakeshole Frying Pan tail.

The Gloucester Birds
(*a found poem from a Twitchers' website*)

Two hundred lapwings at Lightenbrook Lane
Two Little Stint on the Tack Piece
On Court Lake a female Scaup
Four avocets from the Zeiss Hide

At Mallard Pike three goosanders
Two goshawks at New Fancy View
A Marsh Harrier showing well
On a 5-bar gate at Splatt

On the balancing lake a water rail and wagtails
The Dartford warbler east of Tommy Taylor's Lane,
4 Crossbills seen over Crabtree Hill
And a great grey Shrike showing well but flighty

Eagle Owl calling this evening, but distant, intermittent,
Sixty Golden Plover flew north-east
A Ring Ouzel still though shy and elusive
A Cetti's Warbler seen, and 3 more heard

A ringed Common Bulbul in a private garden
Three thousand starlings on the landfill
Nine longtailed tits on the suet balls
Buzzards avoiding ravens in the skies round Paradise

An oystercatcher on The Rushy
Water Pippit on Bottom New Piece floods
At Pit 43 a pair of Smew
A coaltit singing at Pilley

The female Ferruginous Duck
was on the Asian Pen again,
Common Crossbills drinking from a puddle
Four hundred linnets on the setaside field

Two peregrines on pylons
Around the Fox Inn a jay
Great Crested Grebes displaying
A stock dove calling
Three woodpeckers drumming
Eight twitchers ogling
But no partridge in the pear tree.

Clockwork couldn't do it

                          make it
jigger and
                stab like that,
slim tail perking
                    black fatness plumping
like a heart

as its gold bill
                savages
the verge's rummage-sale

   a   met   ro   nome
              among daisies
         less prim than they look
who almost smile at this
          frantic   body
             search
by a guy in leathers
        whose mind is on
   only   one   thing.

The Sighting

A dodo came to Genevieve's allotment.
She was picking runner-beans at the time,
feasting her eyes on a steaming red sun
as it broke through the mist above Toadsmere Wood
so she didn't see the dodo.
That night it was on the local news,
though the sunrise didn't feature.

Witnesses worked out that this rarely-seen creature
must have somehow made its way from the clock-tower
where it was first spotted by a short-sighted old lady
who mistook it for her grandson,
to the disused cemetery where it was captured
on Tom Critchley's mobile phone.
He saw it lumber clumsily —
I felt kinda sorry for it then, he told the lass with the microphone —
down the lane to the Applegarth Allotments
which is precisely where Gen never saw it.

Everybody pestered her at skittles
at The Shearman's Arms that night
but she shrugged it off.
suspected it had something to do with
it being the start of April.

The Visitors

I saw them from the spare room
where nobody's slept for years,
which is only opened for the ironing board
and the Morris Team's money tin.

They were more Mummers Side than Morris.
You'd never catch them dancing
but certainly made a show —
bristled, flounced
like cancan girls in blue.

Two of them, on the flat roof,
picking around like pigeons.
What had I done to deserve this?
What was I on?

I thought I'd better keep quiet,
but the neighbours had seen,
the whole neighbourhood knew.

They stayed around for days,
choosing new places at whim,
until the press got hold.
Escapees from Ozleworth, they said.
They do make off from time to time.
Should we try to catch them?
No need, they'll make their own way back
when the novelty of suburbia grows thin.

Today it would be a hit on Facebook,
with loads more photos than mine
but those were more secretive times,
at least seven years ago now,
about the time I nearly died
but that's another story.

Every time I look out
on that prosaic felted roof
with its silver puddle after rain,
its moss tossed down by birds off the tiling,
I remember those peacocks
and chortle.

Birdsong

Someone traps it with a name before I've heard it –
holds back my flood of words with a raised finger.
It seldom comes again, leaving me excluded
from its hopping eye-cocked world.

Once it was a chiff-chaff, that master of gossip and
onomatopoeia, which I swore I'd never heard,
although I must have, many times.
If to hear is to be conscious, I'm a deaf man,
shut off from a whole dimension.
Clotted ear-wax daft.

Another time it was the dreaded
nightingale, under whose spell a poet fears to fall.
Its fluidity I grant you, and its showmanship
to rival an auctioneer,
and though I have a weakness for the thrush's scurrilous quips.
for me the blackbird reigns supreme.

Today no interpreter was handy.
I sat by a marsh one evening gilded and serene
as a spokesman fenced in a nearby clump
rehearsed his repertoire of passwords.
Attempts to hack its Facebook page were useless,
like annotating Schoenberg live.
It was simpler not to strive, not even dare
to spot it flitting between reeds
or winging its featureless silhouette
against a low dazzling sun.

It was sufficient just to sit,
letting one's blood slip down invisible staves
like raindrops whose colours
glint, flare and darken
as they roll without resistance
from wire to weed to soil.

The pickers

From my bed I see them every morning
commuters, not of clocktime
but following the sun,
and back again at dusk,
gulls
sculling the inland tides of air:
filling the valley like fighters
bound for the killing fields.

Not like the straggle of Poles we passed
trudging back from the fruit farm
to their shack on the edge of the wood.
There are hundreds of these gulls,
a flickering white squadron, sat-navving
as only they know how,
to brown upland furrows
where they settle like pebbles, gravel, grain,
spuming up as the tractor approaches,
feathering its wake, a frayed bridal train.
How dreary ploughland is without them.

At their end-of-day trek, I know where they go.
I've seen them there,
arriving in droves, picnickers
that forage in the silver mud,
then perform again that aerial fan-dance,
a fountain sprayed by the Severn Bore.

The Swans

From day through night the swans are flying;
their carpet-beater wings raise not a speck of dust
as instinctively they imitate each other,
like mime artistes, or that party trick
when everyone crosses legs as if by magic
but the fall guy cannot spot the one to blame.

Gazers-up from underneath their flight path
see a well-drilled formation
a White Arrow Squadron
beating ever west.

Across a sun-bleached lake they flicker,
above a fuming rush-hour town
on through twilight as the lamps appear,
into the cool dark sky of nowhere.

From a tower our satellite device
can track the path they're taking
over pylons, white-fringed coastlines,
through chilling bowls of cloud,
but who'll wear the yellow jersey
for their jagged mountain stretch
is a sleight of hand,
an instinct we can't share.

Poet

When a poet can do what a bar-tailed godwit can do

When he can step alexandrines through mud
while stalking the metaphor lurking down deep in the weed

When he can wait with wind-ruffled plumes
on only one leg
and be ready to strike at whatever may chance

When he can poke his pink scalpel bill
into dark holes that stink
and not stir up slime
but swivel a morsel
and swallow it whole without chomping

When he can break from his sojourn on Humber
to fly in the teeth of a nerve-sapping gale
to the Steppes
just to have sex and return

Yet never mention a thing about it
only hitch up his pants on the scummed edge of tide
and go on picking out pearls

He might deserve our acclaim.

Remembered on hearing Rautavaara

No-one here but us,
paused in our hesitant tread
to listen to the night
and what it brings —
insects melting into twilight,
the marsh seeping,
and the blood-chill snort and trumpet of wild boar
crashing unaware of us,
snouting leaf-mould grubs.

An orchestra is in full swing,
the snare-drum of the nearby forest swishing,
its choir chanting.
Our pause is frozen now;
we are marionettes
suspended between disbelief and awe,
and the vast pomp of the forest
grows darker round our glade
as the crescendo peaks
in a shrill vibrato

through which they come,
dark darts, first two or three
and then a dozen
churring exultation,
scissoring and slitting apart the air
like witchy ballerinas,
no more a figment of our faith
but suddenly everywhere

and we, like bushes, posts
anchored in bracken,
mere nodes of navigation
for the nightjars.

The 14th way of looking at a blackbird
(*in memoriam Gerry Cox*)

For days he has been everywhere,
a party trick, multiplying,
flapping and leaping
from the top hat of the snow
— a dove in negative.

Now, when icicles vanish
like the lady from the box,
when bearers shuffle from the chapel
the deadweight of my friend

I see the blackbird,
undertaker-suited,
peeping from the porchway of the laurel,
his gold bill poised as if to say
It's time to go.

V

Rough day

The tide is rushing out
frantically today
with a gale behind it.
I thought I liked
turbulent water
but only coming in.

Ebbing should be a staid affair.
This urgency's indecent,
a rabble caught in a crush,
cork-coloured heads and pimply necks
straining, straining,

as if they've seen the black leaves
scattered like ashes,
noticed the half-mast flag
struggling to get free,
and they know there's only one place they can go —

the foaming wide-jawed sea.

I should exult in the way
the sandbank's lying naked,
but the force inside the water
is tugging at my skin.

He was the same generation as me.

Last days with Richard

I knew you'd suggest going in as soon as we saw it
lurking behind kerbside cars like a man in dark glasses.

The high street of the old market town
like its namesake ruined castle
was already caving in
to the clamour for Starbucks, Burgerland, Tesco Express,
and two-dimension frontages with scaffolds,
white-faced, being coaxed back from the dead..

You dived into History; I flirted with Poetry;
nothing found to charm our wallets open.
But out of guilt or sense of form I hazarded a fiver
on a memoir set in Exmoor ten counties south.
The shirt-sleeved proprietor seemed mildly bemused
at how we'd shilly-shallied for a pittance
when outside it wasn't even raining.

What I remember best of that day was the local pies we bought
with Dandelion and Burdock for our lunch beside the lake.
Only on reflection do I see it was die-hard habit drew you in
to that emporium of bindings.
The tomes you'd amassed in a lifetime of lecturing and research
weighed too much already, in the months before your death.
One by one, they slipped the leash, to friends, bazaars, Oxfam
— the hindsight fate awaiting all our prized collections.

Stormlight

My tattered road atlas gave you inspiration.
A new Nature Reserve on an old coal shore
where sun warmed the sea foil smooth,
not a wrinkle anywhere.
A late August evening,
four months before your death.

A miners' terrace in that slanting light
cried out for a photo,
but the sky was bruising royal blue,
the wind flicked seagull shadows on our faces
and over towards Saltburn
the sea's brazier cooled
to a rash of silver sparkles.

Back among the scrubby dunes
two boys on bikes
came skidding and whooping.
This evening that they tore through without heeding
could be printed on the soft skin of their minds
to surface unaccountably in age,
as it has for me now,
stirred like those grassheads
by the bowing of your cello.

Veterans

No Great War veterans left.
This old footage takes me back,
not to any trenches but to Blackheath,
my ground-floor bedsit window's view,
a spread of grass and sky.

Albert was my landlord,
shorter even than me
with a "gammy leg."
He got it, he said, from the heat
of his horse's body —
he was in the cavalry,
and "horses' bodies are hundreds of degrees."
Being an ex-milkman he'd have known
horses all his life.
I thought of shovels, steaming muck.

We sat in his kitchen;
he'd made a pot of good brown tea,
set biscuits on a plate.
It only happened once, but he loved to talk.
His rheumy eyes sparkled,
a chuckle in his voice

as he remembered a spy they caught in the woods
who was taken off and shot.
That's all I recall of his yarning,
hot horses and a spy.

Fifty years ago and I've only just remembered him,
hearing these long-dead veterans reminisce.
I feel like a survivor.
Soon,
even those of us they spoke to will be gone.

Two minutes' silence

At eleven o'clock we, the Talking Newspaper readers,
read each others' minds and cease to talk.
Our listeners being a day away,
we do not record this silence.
It could consume vital minutes.

I sit with closed eyes and listen.
John Cage all over again.
The woman beside me coughs.
My head abuzz with newsreels of the Somme.
And her coughing becomes theirs,
the silence something deeper,
thick as a pall of smoke.

When a pretence of normality returns,
we will joke to break the tensions.
Brian will read the obituaries.
I think of our listeners, many sightless,
who do not need this silence.

Penultimate Act

He's been in that place down the road
for eleven weeks now
and won't come home again.
He'll soon be out of it, they both know that.
So she's made an early start,
not bothering what the neighbours think.
She's not from round here anyway.

Apart from what he might have left
stuffed under the mattress,
this is her inheritance, on public display,
a growing tangled heap in a roadside skip.
Passing its gaping jaw each afternoon
I note its changing diet.
First, tied-up bags of dusty magazines,
cakes in packets with last year's sell-by dates;
a dozen biscuit tins;
today, old radios, their cables dangling,
upthrust legs of chairs,

I'm beginning to see what I'm at in there she says
as we meet along the path,
pushing back untended hair
with a smeared hand.
A couple more days should do it.

It was evening.
A yellow light shone out
from dusty upstairs windows
for the first time in years.

Fencing

Frank and myself kept it patched and propped between us.
It leaned, buckled, had gaps beneath
that I called hedgehog routes.
The fence to the south was a proper job,
erected for Gwen by a man from up yonder.
The crumpled one was down to me
but Frank had no complaints,
my tenant, and equally tight-fisted.

On his death I sold the place
to a fellow in his thirties
who loves nothing so much as
gravel and renewal.
A smart new fence was part of the deal.

Last week they became a small park,
our two plots with nothing between.
Three days I relished the space, the light,
then concrete posts went in.
They stood in a measured line like guards
hands behind their backs,
warning of things to come.

Today the sound of sawing;
two panels in already.
Soon they will all join hands and
stride down to the lane.
It makes sense; the old one shamed us,
testament to neglect.
Now I live with the sort of bounds
that decent people do.
But I've never been keen to keep order.
It's like owning the Berlin Wall.

All I can say is I've got a good neighbour
who did a fine job at minimal cost,
and a good fence it is that's gone up between us.
(I've not asked him if he's heard of Robert Frost.)

My goat-willow tree

I admit it's not the sort of tree a gardener would grow –
my neighbour, hinting, says she thinks it was self-seeded.
And her cocky fence-contractor, brandishing his bow-saw
had the nerve to ask if the wretched thing was needed.
"O reason not the need" I thought, and was pushed to disagree
when he condemned it as a hazard, too rampant a thing
to have growing near a house… though it is more a weed than tree.
But in my hill-shaded garden it's a telegraph of Spring
and to its forks each winter a robin comes to sing;

Leafless and unbudded on this January day
with its dark latticed branches etched against the sky
like shreds of rusted swarf on a tarnished metal tray,
its scaffolding suits the blackbird, whose hunger-sharpened eye
acts as a green signal to every bird nearby.
Soon an avian menagerie is fussing in its boughs:
chaffinch, dunnock, thrush and a cute if ragged titmouse
perch like quavers on a stave. (The wren, discreetly shy,
prefers more private shelter in a shrub against the house).

I don't love but I respect my arboreal mongrel,
this tin-man scrapyard puppet, with limbs like armaments
and acid-green hair that in Autumn shrinks to shrapnel.
Its roots are with the dead but its head is in the firmament.
I could live on a new estate and breed an ornamental
cherry-tree that primps itself with pink fluff in its hair.
But there's didikoi in my nature. A primitive fundamentally,
I'm ill-at-ease in salons, or in any quarter where
Art tends to the lavish or deliberately spare.

What I like most is its hardiness, the way it allows me
to slash it each October, cut it to the quick,
while cursing it for the shadow it casts upon my house,
how it shreds the garden's sunlight. I think I've trumped its trick
as like some grisly surgeon I gather up the thicket
of twigs and torn branches for the council's mulching skip.
But trashed thus, is it timid, have I stalled its wayward streak?
Not so. Next spring, as ever, it lets liquid voltage rip
and against my neighbour's phone-line it flicks a scornful tip.

Such days

He — or is it she ? — has had a haircut.
My neighbour praised its shape —
in milk-gold light a sibyl dancing;
the muscular limbs that had cradled me
look graceful now, balletic,
a cello-bowing pose.

Frank had called instructions from below
to me whose long-armed sharp-lipped shears
lacked navigation, due sense of proportion.
It was like my own postponed operation.
Tree-surgeon — how apt a phrase!

From its leaf-mottled height I scanned the hills,
the sweep of lane and gardens.
Wind-chimes clattered as I clambered.
Nothing else ruffled their silver pinions
on this morning of no breeze.

I leaned against nubbled forks and drank the air,
a Green Man at peace in autumn's ease,
on a swingboat stilled at the close of the fair.
Such days are heaven-sent for trimming trees.

Busy day at the Beaufort

I was in The Beaufort Arms,
waiting for my faggots
when a man came in to arrange a wake.
What if it were mine?
He didn't know it was me sitting there
and in a way it wasn't.

I heard him tell the licensee
the funeral would be at St Jude's church
a mile away down Quarry Lane.
All my forebears are buried there,
their headstones unreadable now,
their table-tombs capsizing,
But I know where they live.

When he left, I sat and wrote
the invitations —
a fine way of passing faggot-warming time
while sipping a well-kept ale.
A cask of this should float me on my way.

Sorted just in time.
A young lad sets a plate before me
with "Careful now, it's hot."
Greedily I eat,
cramming body and soul together.

Time to leave.
It nearly always is.
You have to plan these things.
The function room is vacant now,
the mourners done and dusted,
their leavings in the bin.
The car park wet and empty.
The sky is a bag of rain.

Shaved

The one time I was shaved without a mirror
it was like being skinned,
my trimmings binned and thrown away,
and everybody cheering, clapping;
even cameras flashed.
I was a peeled spud, a pencil fresh sharpened,
broke waves among my colleagues
with my felon's shaven head.

I kept myself under wraps,
as a sort of birthday present;
two hours before I took a peek.
"There's a man at the door"
I heard my daughter say
as the window threw me back,
a smoke-grey freak.

Because I hadn't looked, I couldn't know
the change they'd wrought in me,
but her grandmother saw at once
the self I'd cut away,
accepting my blank mask
in the spirit she once viewed
her husband's coffined stare.

But I could see at once
I was not my daughter's kin,
not having been smooth-jawed
since she was born.
I watched her own jaw drop,
hands rise to her face
as though to feel if she had been transformed,
before those hands reached up
for a reassuring hug.

Being young she soon adapted,
almost forgave me, almost
saw me as her father,
but I,
I had to turn away
from every shop, from every plate-glass showroom
in the town's weird hall of mirrors
day after haunted day.

"How can you be sure that you are the 17th reincarnation of the Buddha?" "Certainly it is very difficult."
   (Radio Four interview)

Being myself the second reincarnation of Ivor Gurney —
the first having died in infancy during the Bristol Blitz —
I put up my hand to moments of doubt.

It's not just the sense of kinship
when I read his "Collected Letters" — most readers share that —
nor the sense when walking from Kings to Maisemore
that I've been this way before.

It's more the urge to cry
"To Hell with it" and sling one's hook,
to say more to beech trees on Portway
than to family and friends,

and the messy scores, the way one's poems
peter out in a tangle like paths from Framilode
(excitement bordering on incoherence),
the tendency to vow there'll be no more cant,
to reply to authority,
"No, I don't think I could."

My reasons to doubt?
I'd never set fire to bedsheets
or be seen at soprano recitals,
least of all in a Severn pilot's coat.
And I'd tell any ghost of Ludwig to
bugger off.

The clincher is more visceral.
Up Barton Street from Botherways,
a newer bakery he never knew
crams my guts with its drippers
and Gurney cries within.

"He's better at being me than I am"
(from an interview on Radio Four)

He used to sit and watch me like a dog.
I'm not much of an actor, least of all as myself.
I can just about manage bank-clerks and trees.
But he's got me to a T,
and knows my every gesture off by heart.

Now often we can't tell us from each other.
If we'd been auditioned for life
he'd have got my part.
What motivates him? Envy ? Admiration ?
Is he a succubus ?

One day he came off set, right past me
as if I wasn't there.
I daren't look in a mirror just in case I wasn't.
Then I noticed disconcertingly
how everyone ignored me.

Suddenly I pictured him walking into my house
to kiss my wife and children.
Would they be glad, I wondered.
I looked up his address,
conjecturing it could work in reverse.

I passed it late last night
and looked up at his window,
Yes, there I was,
a thin sketch on the curtains,
leaning towards another
shapely silhouette.

That holiday was card games

15/2 the rest won't do
15/4 the rest won't score
the joy of finding 13 in The Box
but never the impossible 19
that Harry liked to claim

We scribbled the scores on envelopes
a rucksack sort of making-do
But here, we have a pegboard,
a caravan fold-up making-do
but nevertheless a pegboard

I'm teaching a rookie how to
sort lay peg
and spot an oppo's double-bluff

She flings pips across the table
"Six" she declares
"Seven" I correct,
"Jack's nob."

I watch and fidget as she ups a stick
and plods one-legged towards home.
I hope she'll get into it one day,
that 5-at-a-time hopscotch,
that longjump into the sand,
as a swan lands on water.

I long to see her grow fluent
as the fanned hands fly,
blithely calling out their names —
Pair o' bigheads
Paddy's Orchard
as sure of their statistics
as Bewick swans returning each fall.

I long for the time
when by her moves
she shows she knows the steps
of the crazy dance
that's cribbage.

To the man who put food out for the badgers

And to think we were so pleased
as you would have been
after Sharon had given them email ear-ache for weeks
at their coming that morning
with mattocks, saw and strimmers.

Air abuzz with their hi-vis labour;
everything uprooted:
the leaning fence and brambles,
jungle-dark laurel so long my foe,
the stunted sun-starved mountain ash,
all at one fell swoop.

They took my breath away, swiped away my smiling.
Where will the blackbird nest this year?
Who could face this stump-scarred bank?
Certainly not you.

If your ghost ever drifted down this lane
feeding as you once did the badger and the fox,
it won't any more,

though yesterday when the breeze was stirring
the wind-chimes on my willow,
I thought I heard a sound I'd never heard before,
though God knows you had cause enough.
It sounded like you weeping.

At "The Bell and Gavel"

I'd never considered there was a technique
or any sort of knack. But it seems there was.
I heard three blokes describing it last week
in The Salutation, and I was riveted, because
a tight-wrapped wire of memory suddenly unravelled
and there I was with the chained ball in my hand
thirty years ago at The Bell and Gavel.
I remembered how, to topple the last man standing,
you had to stoop, squint and let the missile go
in an apparently wrong direction
so that it swung like a skater in a slow
graceful arc, and you stretched up in satisfaction
as you watched it swerve in like a googlie, whack,
then with a hollow wooden clattering sound
the Last of The Mohicans was sprawling on his back,
spinning over the ledge, and rolling round and round,
while every bloke was clapping, or sorting out change
to buy you a Black and Tan or a Mild and Bitter,
whatever took your fancy, because you, a stranger,
had taught them what it takes to be The Killer.

Vinyl Albums

It took 3 months to play
one by one
my hundred vinyl albums

the oldest going back
thirty years,
acquisitions lost in fog.

I dusted them, baptised them
at the sink
and dried them like frail babies.

When I sat and listened,
what I heard
was my crystal history.

I seemed to smell the rain,
smoke, tarmac
of the times I first heard them

and listening I became
who I was,
restoring a blood kinship,

almost a wilful self-
drowning, when
all one's lost days ripple by.

To slow that sensation,
to have it
by the tail, held and relished,

to wrap it round and round,
a wool scarf
with all its tobacco taints

was a rare way to spend
an evening
of searing, too early frost.

"Silver dew on the bluegrass"

Frost was visible everywhere that night,
intensifying the white billows as the steam locomotive
barked up a Shropshire bank,
filling moonlit field with coffins
as our carriage-lights flicked by.

Home was in darkness. Inside the chill gripped hard.
With trembling hands, I read the note on the table.

The next day I would visit you,
staring from your bed with one blank eye,
in that ward so fuggy I threw up on the floor.
But for now I found stale biscuits,
brewed a pot of tea,
and just to fend off silence,
selected an LP.

Tonight I take again
that black vinyl plate from its crumpled sleeve
for the first time in five decades.

More scratches than I'd reckoned on, more dust
as the stylus drags its leg around the curves.
But above the static hiss of years,
their voices rise in harmony
like a pair of doves set free.

"In the days that used to be
How I wish that you could see
Silver dew on the blue grass tonight."

I can't imagine those magnolias,
that lonely girl a-riding.
A rime lies round my heart
and all I can see
is a dim front passage, its dust-coated bulb
chasing shadows like roaches
that creep beneath the skirting.

One Way Street

The place we want is up a one-way street
in an unfamiliar town. First left, we're told,
but not from this end. True to form, we meet
a dustcart and a truck delivering coal
at the other. When we're through, the forecourt's
chocabloc, the street double-yellow-lined.
At Reception, we're studiedly ignored
while a chap with trade-plates and overalls signs
a stack of carbon-copies.
                        "Dropping or collecting?"
she asks at last. "We're fully booked this week, though."
My name's an undropped penny. "I'm the wrecked
green Clio. Come for my CD's. If you'd
show me where it is, I'll…" Her green eyes fix me.
"It's gone, luv. Crushed. But we did save your tax disc."

Markers
(*for Alison and Ettie*)

There's a milestone on the byway skirting Whitestone Hill
protected by a sturdy fence from 4x4's and plough
that serves no current purpose, just a curiosity now.
Summertime, half-lost in Queen Anne's Lace and Cranesbill,
and pelted in Autumn by the spreader spattering dung,
it has spurned all efforts at uprooting, a survivor –
a bee-skep with no entrance; a hillfort's welded shive;
the outcrop of an underworld; proboscis; larva; tongue.

Now no-one takes this ancient route from Wells to Salisbury,
how many hours for hoof or shank its wrinkles don't betray,
though on sleek fresh-laid tarmac a dozen miles away
sat-navs calibrate each wheelspin along the A303.

High and dry by this old stone above the winding Stour
my gaze can sketch a ley-line from your skull to Alfred's Tower.

The hulks' graveyard
(for fellow-painter Barry Hill)

I seem sucked to this land between waters
that clings to its shelf with spindle claws.

The buttressed world's unreachable –
a jetty's thumbstall, or square-mouthed cave
of the far shore's tunnel where a train
like a caterpillar blithely jinks away.

Here are only shifting margins,
hostages to the warring tides:
shrinking red wet islands
where oystercatchers strut,
furrows of brown water on the move.

Clouds come here to fatten, pale and shrink —
sharp air glitters like a rink
with the blown spume of plover.

These bones were meant to hold it all together,
wrinkled ribs of timber, sunk
in coarse grass thick as fur.

Afternoon sky in South Gloucestershire

Morning's earnestness has been shunted away
and after lunch the carnival prepares.
In the corners of skyfields, the entries gather:
fluffy princesses, blue-suit marching bands, the hosts
of chivvying officials. A silver show in bright spots,
but sagging bags of water dumped around in case of need
show nothing's out of the question.
                              This is a sky that
remembers years past, however unique today.
Ever since time was mooted by planning committees,
dates on calendars, children desperate for the holiday,
this sky has gathered its wardrobe: chiffon, pinstripe,
summer's glad-rags, winter's woollen mufflers.

My mind has shot snaps from as many angles
as it can manage in excitement, if excitement is the word
for those minutes when the bottle empties
and the cigar withers in its groove.

Suddenly it can't keep up. The band has switched
from tuning-up to marching, and the carnival is on me,
puddles forming all around my eyes, crowfooted with the drops
that sweep across leaves, grass-blades, fence-wire.
The flat felt roof is a ballroom now, of
leaping widening rings, like soundwaves from a mast,
and the afternoon sky of Gloucestershire fades
to a monochrome strip at the end of a used-up film.

November Dusk
(a Keatsian ode)

An arc of watery gold has been leached from the sky
and the hill with its fleecy crest is a smudge of shade
as my window fills with the fifth storm of the day.
Its jewels, once tears, become streaks of a silver blade.
The goat-willow tree that shakes in its ragged coat
is a ball-bearing maze where winter's first chaffinch
tightens her grip on a glossy black bough.
Tossed like a fairground swing-boat
the tangled wind-chime's tune grows frantic now,
rhythm and melody snatched by a fractured branch.

Here in my armchair, lapped by Classic FM
as it waterfall-tumbles from Gershwin to Strauss
I can't decide which adagio to hum.
A percussion brushed on the drumskin of the house
is stringing me taut, too heedful of the rain's
toneless static, and the tree's conductor wand
wagging against the grim face of the sky.
These, and the wind-chime's mania,
tug at my mind like a boat lashed up in the bay
swung by each gust between spray and sea and land.

Crepuscule

Round here we don't have many nights like this.
One I remember — little short of midnight —
the woods banked up, shaggy-black,
a hive of owls against a forest lake.

But even that was not like this
Pienkowski patchwork
where veins of leaf and ragged oak-bark edge
are pressed into a putty sky
like sweaty fingerprints.

Bronze rain above,
fine siftings of the stars
filtered through foliage;

below, a sooty mist
is rising from the leafmould,
all Time's stillage
heaving up its rocks and roots.

And one old tree, thick-waisted,
its thatch a scarecrow's,
crooks a finger at the moon
that dips its horns beneath a crest,
declining to surrender.

Redemption

It's on these autumn afternoons

when the bee agog on the buddleia,
the flush of the neighbour's drain,
the siren from the highway over the hill,
and the string quartet on the hi-fi
through the summer-wide window
seem parts of a larger symphony

that I'm quite prepared to die.

The bird-table is a Gallician *horreo,*
gold-teak one side, sinister the other,
and on the goat-willow
some leaves are lucent, others dry
and rolled for smoking.

The geranium is napping between blooms,
the lawn half straw, half clover,
and gnats have come to jive to the string quartet.

The carnival's not over
but this is the final dance
when everything joins in.

My soul — whatever hat it's wearing —
stands on the touchline watching,
not concerned if The Ref has got it wrong.

Even the goblet tells me
I have known such fulfilment
as only a sleep will redeem

and such a moment need never come again.

Threshold

When darkness is filling the streets
apart from the lamps
with their haloes of mist
smouldering orange or a ghostly blue

a door may open
blessing a doorstep with light
and a shadow's voice call softly
the name of a cat or child

as if this threshold
were a harbour wall
and all beyond a black sea
with no boats coming in

Stand here a while
as a can or paper skitters
and a small wind rustles
the skirts of the trees

and before turning back
to the sham death of sleep,
sip and savour the night air,
lose count of those elusive stars.

Notes and Acknowledgements

p15: *Westerly* — first published in 'The Road to Cherington' (Kingscourt Press, 2008)

p21: *Mind Shop 5* — 'scallies': scallywags.

p21: *Mind Shop 6* — 'Scruggs rolls' an iconic finger sequence on the 5-string banjo, named after its inventor, the Bluegrass legend Earl Scruggs.

p27: *God Willing* — originally appeared in 'South' magazine under a different title.

p 30: *Things our art teacher* – several teachers used to exclaim of a noisy class: 'It's like a bear garden in here!'

p37: *Hartley Everett* — catching elvers was once a common pastime around Gloucester in Spring. 'Weskit' is Westgate Bridge over The Severn.

p38: *For Robbie MacGregor* — a verbatim obituary from a national newspaper. The dedicatee was, as far as I know, not related to the subject.

p42: *I Call her Myra* — readers should take to heart the wording of the final stanza!

p47: *Tom Warwick's book* —all essentially true apart from names and the last 2 stanzas

p48: *The Fine Art Collector* — an almost verbatim recall of a rant in France.

p56: *Sainsbury Sequence (i)* — A study by Francis Bacon for a portrait of Vincent V.G.

p61: *That Shed* — I felt this worked without the need to mention Dylan Thomas.

p65: *"View from Madron Cross"* — Alfred Wallis was a so-called naïve painter and fisherman taken up by St Ives artists such as Ben Nicholson. He died in poverty in Madron workhouse in 1942.

p66: *In a Bar in Madron* — *Oche* is defined as "the line behind which the thrower must stand in playing darts," and is pronounced *ockie*.

p67: *As she tells it* — a true reminiscence by a friend who was a girl in St Ives during World War 2. The gasworks she saw bombed is now the Tate Gallery.

p68: *Bolitho's* — 'a double carpet' is betting slang for the odds of 33-1. There is a legend explaining its origin. In 1876 Oliver Corn placed a bet with odds 33/1, because he needed money to purchase a carpet.

p69: *Penzance Pirates* — an event on Mazey Day, the revived Feast of Goljowan, which also provided the title for the following poem.

p72: *Collage from a Cornish Guest Book* — Many thanks to the highly literate guests whose entries over the years unwittingly helped create these poems. This poem and *Field, Chynoweth Lane* are dedicated to Emily and Damian.

p78: *The Gloucester Birds* — thanks to those who posted any of these phrases on the 'Gloucester Birder' website.

p80: *Clockwork couldn't do it* — The description of the blackbird in this poem was influenced by Ted Hughes' phrase about the thrush: "more coiled steel than living".

p86: *The Swans* — selected for 'South' magazine, April 2020.

p87: *Poet* — first appeared in 'Getting the Bird' with paintings by Neil Griffiths, published by Prospect Press, 2008.

p88: *Remembered on Hearing Rautavaara* — I had all but forgotten my one encounter with nightjars until asked to respond to a recording of Rautavaara's 'Cantus Articus'.

p89: *The 14th way of looking at a blackbird* — The title is a nod to Wallace Stevens' much-imitated poem *13 Ways of Looking at a blackbird*.

p92: *Rough day* — The final line does not refer back to any other poem. The deceased who sprang to mind on this occasion was not personally known to me.

p94: *Stormlight* — first published in 'South' magazine, April 2020.

p98: *Fencing* — The last line refers to Robert Frost's "Good fences make good neighbours".

p108: *That Holiday was Card Games* — based on an attempt to teach a lady cribbage. Any puzzling phrases indicate that the reader is equally unfamiliar with the scoring and pegboard systems of the game, too many to explain. But "Jack's nob" is ergot for the extra point scored when you hold a Knave of a certain suit ; the Box is the bonus hand that alternates between players; it is apparently impossible to score 19, though not 17,18, 20,21, so Harry would fling a zero hand down on the table and shout "19".

p111: *At 'The Bell and Gavel'* — Table skittles of the sort described was once a popular game at pubs such as the one in the title, named after the local cattle market. Black and Tan and Mild and Bitter were popular beer mixes.

p118: *The hulks' graveyard* — a wonderful spot on the banks of the tidal Lower Severn where old barges and trows were beached to prevent erosion. This poem was awarded Second Prize in a Chipping Sodbury Poetry Competition. Trust me!

p122: *Redemption* — *horreos* are raised granaries traditional to Galicia in North-west Spain.

David Ashbee

David Ashbee was one of the first new poets published by Enitharmon Press in 1989, with *Perpetual Waterfalls*. A member of Cherington Poets and Cheltenham Poetry Society, he has regularly performed in schools and festivals, and at Holub, the Severnside poetry group he has run for 30 years. He reviews new poetry for 'South' magazine, in which his own work frequently appears.